≫ 52 ≪

WAYS TO HELP

YOUR CHILD
DO BETTER IN
SCHOOL

»52«
WAYS TO HELP
YOUR CHILD
DO BETTER IN
SCHOOL

Jan Dargatz

OLIVER
NELSON

Thomas Nelson Publishers
Nashville

Published in Nashville, Tennessee, by Oliver-Nelson Books, a division of Thomas Nelson, Inc., Publishers, and distributed in Canada by Word Communications, Ltd., Richmond, British Columbia.

Printed in the United States of America.

Library of Congress Cataloging-in-Publication Data

Dargatz, Jan Lynette.
    52 ways to help your child do better in school / Jan Dargatz.
        p.   cm.
    ISBN 0-8407-9662-5
    1. Home and school—United States.   2. Education—United States—Parent participation.   3. Parent and child—United States.
I. Title.   II. Title: Fifty-two ways to help your child do better in school.
LC225.3.D37   1993
649'.68—dc20   93-19141
                                                                CIP

        1   2   3   4   5   6   —   98   97   96   95   94   93

To

Mrs. Hodges
Mrs. McKillip
Mrs. Senior
Miss Fee
and
Mrs. Hardwick
teachers who taught me about teaching

● Contents

Introduction

Only *part*—albeit a significant part—of your child's education happens in school. Whether at home, in a private setting, or on a public campus, school helps your child learn various subjects and teaches learning skills. School helps your child with socialization behaviors and teaches your child how and when to cooperate and compete. School exposes your child to topics and equipment previously unexplored in daily life. School makes available learning tools and books that may not be accessible in any other setting. School provides a systematic means of leading your child from one level of intellectual development and skill to another.

As a formal, institutionalized approach to learning, school is basic and vital. But . . . your child does not limit learning to school hours. To your child, all of life is a "school." Every event is educational. Every encounter is instructive. Every new experience teaches—for good or bad, to greater or lesser degrees, with measurable or immeasurable results.

As a parent, you have the ability to affect your child's formal schooling process in many ways. Your greater role and privilege, however, are to influence the eight to ten hours a day that your child is *not* in school but is still learning.

Not all teachers are parents. But every parent—and

every grandparent—is a teacher. This book provides suggestions for becoming a more effective teacher during out-of-school hours and for making the out-of-school experiences ones that enhance, support, and extend the schooling process.

1 • Talk Positively About School

Your child knows he *has* to go to school. How he feels about going to school, however, is something that will be determined to a great extent by how *you* feel about schooling.

If you say to your child, "I didn't like going to school either when I was your age," your child will approach school as something negative that must be endured.

If you say to your child, "Math was my worst subject," you are setting your child up to expect failure in math.

If you say to your child, "Weekends are the best, aren't they?" you are likely to have a child who spends many hours in school daydreaming about the upcoming weekend or what she would do if she were at home.

Be strongly positive about your child's schooling opportunities. Emphasize the importance of attending school and learning as much as possible. Be enthusiastic as you send your child off to school in the morning:

- "I can hardly wait to hear all about what you learn today."

- "Do your best and learn as much as you can."

- "Isn't learning fun?"

School is your child's "work." Just as you prepare to face a day of chores and challenges, so your child faces a day of problem solving, learning new concepts, trying out new skills, and working in new ways with peers and adults. Be as positive about *your* day as you are about your child's day:

- "Well, we're both off to conquer new worlds! We'll be together this afternoon to compare notes."

- "I've got a lot to do today. So do you. Let's learn as much as we can and do the best we can. Ready . . . set . . . let's go!"

- "It's Monday! We finally get to go back to school and work!"

In setting a positive tone about school, you are reinforcing what most children feel as an intuitive "high" about learning. Children naturally love to learn. They love to explore, to create, to see how much they can do and accomplish. Children are born with an appetite for discovery and conquest. It's up to us as parents and caring adults to nourish that natural trait, not squelch it.

Furthermore, children with a positive attitude about schooling tend to have better attendance records, to be more eager to try new things or acquire new skills, to be more open to learning new concepts, and to display fewer behavior problems. In turn, children who show these traits tend to score higher on tests and to engage more in small group discussions and activities. In sum, the child who is positive about school does better in school!

Your child will draw most of her feelings about school from you. Be pro school in everything you say and do.

2 • Choose Your Child's School

Today, schooling options are much broader and more accessible than they were only two decades ago. Many large Protestant churches offer schooling of some type. Montessori and private community schools are increasingly popular. Home-schooling curriculums are readily available, as are community-based home-schooling associations. Even within public school districts, parents are frequently given a choice about which school their child might attend.

Question Time   Become fully informed about your schooling options. Here are several questions to ask as you research the possibilities:

1. Is this school safe for my child? Your child's physical well-being and emotional safety are paramount factors.

2. Does this school reinforce the values of our family? Will the child be learning concepts and behaviors at school that are opposite to what we may be teaching at home?

3. What are the educational standards that have been set—and with what results? Ask questions about standardized test performance. Ask to see the textbooks being used. Discuss the curriculum being taught at your child's grade level.

4. How are the classrooms and class schedules structured? Your child may need a disciplined, teacher-intensive approach more than a free-floating, open-classroom, self-motivated approach—or vice versa. Your child may do better in a school with one teacher for all subjects or many teachers, each specialized.

5. What is the relationship between teachers and children? The best way to get a feel for this is to sit in on a class or two. Are the teachers overly strict? Strict enough? Do they encourage discussion? Do the classrooms reflect creative activity?

Choose Your Child's Teacher   Within a school, do your utmost to choose your child's teacher. How can you go about this?

- Attend open house evenings. After you have visited your child's classroom(s), wander over to the classrooms of the next grade. Talk to some of the teachers. Look at the work and projects being displayed. Observe how the children converse with their teachers. Ask questions of a teacher. After all, you might be entrusting your child to his care for more than a thousand hours next year!

- Make a fifteen-minute appointment with the principal. Express your concern about your child's progress. Discuss any special needs of your child. If you desire that your child be placed in the classroom of a specific teacher (or teachers), say so.

A Fresh Start   Sometimes a change in school is a positive move for a child, especially if he has faced early developmental problems or has had to learn how to compensate for learning disabilities. A new school can provide a fresh start in overcoming behavioral problems or even problems associated with a child's perception of himself as a "failure."

Continuity   On the other hand, sometimes staying in the "old school," even if the family (or part of the family) has moved to a new neighborhood, is a stabilizing factor for a child in a time of upheaval, such as a divorce. Make your *child's* educational welfare top priority in deciding whether to remain or switch.

Even a Year or Two   Occasionally, parents may be unable to sustain a long-term commitment to home schooling or private schooling, but they can provide a year or two of intensive training at home or the opportunity to attend a private or special-emphasis school. Go for it! Make your child's educational experience the best you can each year.

3 • Develop a Relationship with Your Child's Teacher

Get to know your child's teacher, and let the teacher get to know you.

When you pick up your child at school, sometimes go all the way to the classroom door. Greet the teacher by name. Give a word of encouragement:

• "Thank you for all you are doing for my son."

• "Thank you for taking extra effort in helping my daughter learn that concept."

Periodically send a note of encouragement to the teacher:

• "My son has never enjoyed school as much as he is enjoying it this year."

• "I see great progress in my daughter's ability to read. Thank you!"

If your child is going through a difficult adjustment or if your family is undergoing a crisis, explain to your child's teacher what is happening.

If a teacher tells you about a problem your child is having, ask, "What do you suggest I do?" Don't become defensive or feel affronted. The teacher is expressing concern and is attempting to *help* your child.

No Wedges   Some children attempt to manipulate the relationship between teacher and parent, just as they attempt to manipulate the relationship between Mom and Dad. Don't let it happen!

On the other hand, if your child tells you of explicit instances of abuse—verbal harassment, physical abuse, sexual impropriety, or browbeating criticism—listen intently. Take her comments seriously. Ask questions. Get as many details as you can. Let your child know that you love her and that you *will* take action. If you suspect that any school employee is abusing your child, go immediately to the school principal and confront the issue. (If the principal is the abuser, go to the superintendent.)

Parent-Teacher Conferences   Periodic formal conferences between parent and teacher—usually one a semester—are for your *child's* benefit. Make them a priority. Listen closely to what the teacher expresses as your child's strengths and weaknesses. Ask how you can bolster the weaknesses. Don't limit your conversation to your child's academic progress. Ask about physical, social, and emotional development.

Ally or Foe?   Most often, your child's teacher will be your strong ally in helping your child grow and develop mentally and emotionally. In the rare instances in which you feel that a teacher is *not* on your side 100 percent, attempt to resolve the situation. Ask the teacher if you can sit in on a class session. Talk to other parents whose children may be having a similar problem. Meet with the teacher directly to discuss your concerns.

If the situation doesn't improve, discuss the situation with the principal. If necessary, request that your child be moved to another classroom. Face problems head-on and resolve them quickly so that your child's education does not suffer.

4 • Attend Open House Functions

The event may be called Parent's Night, Open House, or School Fair. Whatever the name, the intent is the same—to give you an opportunity to see your child's school from the inside out, to meet your child's teacher(s), and to let your child show off her work and introduce her friends. Be there.

If at all possible, make the event an all-family event with both parents and all children in attendance. Let your child take the lead. It is his opportunity to "show and tell."

Be sure to meet your child's teacher. Ask general questions. This occasion is *not* the time to raise specific concerns about your child or to point out problems you perceive.

Talk to other parents, perhaps for purposes of arranging a car pool, play group, party, or sports team. But keep conversations with adults to a minimum.

Look carefully at the work, displays, and projects your child calls to your attention. Ask questions about what you see. Applaud his efforts. In attending an open visitation function and in expressing genuine interest in your child's school and progress, you are sending a strong signal to him that school is important to you. The more important school is to you, the more important it will be to him.

Get-Acquainted Functions   Some schools hold an "open" day prior to the beginning of a school year so that students (and parents) can meet teachers, perhaps make a new friend or two, and find their classrooms before the first day of class. By all means, attend! These events are especially significant if your child is attending a new school.

School Performances   The school pageant or play. The annual spring concert. The after-school soccer match. The schoolwide art show. Whenever possible, be there! Be an enthusiastic and ardent fan. Don't criticize your child's effort or performance. Don't compare your child to others in the group. Appreciate what your child has done, is doing, and will do!

5 • Help Out at Your Child's School

Most schools provide opportunities for parents to assist as teacher's aides. Some private schools *require* this assistance from parents to keep tuition costs down!

As an aide, you may be asked to read to children or listen to them read, to grade papers, to help out with maintaining discipline, to provide one-on-one remedial help, to take attendance, to duplicate papers, or to create bulletin board displays.

Being an aide allows you to get a close-up view of your child's schooling progress:

- You'll see how your child relates to the teacher. Is she free to ask questions and make comments? Does the teacher pay her too much attention or too little? Does she speak to the teacher with respect?

- You'll see how much fear your child has regarding the learning process. Is he afraid of making mistakes? Of trying something new? Of asking a question? Of taking a test?

- You'll see how your child relates to her peers. Is she a bully? A doormat? A domineering talker? A leader? A cooperative colleague?

- You'll discover areas in which your child is strong and areas in which your child is weak. These often aren't registered by report cards or a survey of his homework. How well does he express himself verbally in front of his class? Does he listen intently or spend most of his time staring out the window?

You are not likely to make these discoveries during your first stint as an aide or even first two volunteer periods. They will come about as the result of periodic participation in the classroom.

Your child may be a bit uptight the first time you appear in his classroom as a teacher's aide. As time passes, however, he'll be more comfortable with your presence and be more natural in his behavior.

Room Mothers or Fathers   Many schools call on parents to plan holiday-related parties or to accompany classes on field trips. Perhaps you can take off a half day twice a year to spend time with your child and her classmates.

Parents Are Number One!

Recent research reveals that parent involvement does more to improve the quality of an elementary school than any other single factor—including generous budget, location of school, quality of facilities, and teacher credentials.

Schools with widespread parent involvement are schools that have fewer disciplinary problems, better maintained facilities, greater morale among students and teachers, and higher standardized test scores!

If parents are not actively involved in *your* child's school, take the lead!

Talk to other parents in your child's class. You might want to hold an evening meeting in your home or to meet some of them for lunch. Discuss the importance of being involved in the schooling process. Talk about ways in which you would be willing individually or collectively to be more active or visible at the school.

Then set up an appointment with your child's teacher or principal. Take two or three other parents with you. Express your interest and explain what you'd like to do. Rarely will your offer be turned down, and if it is, ask why.

Parent involvement should include both moms and dads whenever possible. It should be periodic and regular, not a onetime event. And it should be a coordinated effort with a mutual understanding of goals, roles, and responsibilities among parents and between parents and teachers.

6 • Read with Your Child

Perhaps no single activity bears as much educational fruit as that of a parent reading with a child. So, pull your child close and open a book.

Read to Your Child No child is too young to be read to—even a newborn. A child will come to identify these times as intensely personal, pleasurable, and positive. Hold your young child as you read to him. Explore the story together.

Choose a variety of materials. Introduce your child to poetry. Read Bible stories. Explore together a children's encyclopedia, including entries about science, history, and other nations. Find biographies written at a child's level of famous people you consider to be good role models.

Avoid reading suspenseful or action-oriented stories at bedtime. They tend to stimulate the imagination and keep a child awake. Familiar tales are best for rereading at bedtime.

No child is too old to be read to. Generally speaking, however, you'll find yourself reading to your older children in these ways:

- sharing unusual fact or opinion excerpts from a newspaper or magazine.

- sharing funny stories, jokes, or amusing tidbits of information.

- sharing thought-provoking quotes or Scriptures.

Reading to your child

- spawns an interest in reading.

- helps your child develop a keener awareness of and appreciation for words and the ways in which language can be used.

- triggers your child's imagination.

- expresses the connection between ideas and words, and helps your child see that much of learning is related to words and the ability to read.

- lets your child know that you value books and ideas.

Let Your Child Read to You As your child learns to read, let her read to you daily. She'll learn to read with greater fluency and increased expression. She'll comprehend more of what she reads. She'll have an immediate association of reward for her reading (your presence), and she'll feel a sense of accomplishment at having read!

Encourage your child to read billboards, store signs, posters, brochures, road signs, can and box labels in the grocery stores, washing instructions on clothing labels, recipes from cookbooks—virtually anything he comes across. Let him experience firsthand the direct relationship between an ability to read and an ability to function fully in society.

In nearly all cases, the more a child reads, the better a child reads . . . the better a child reads, the more a child enjoys reading . . . the more a child enjoys reading, the more a child learns from reading . . . the more a child learns from reading, the more a child enjoys reading . . . and so on. An upward learning spiral is created.

7 • Take Your Child to the Library

A library card is your child's passport to an entire world of ideas.

Go to the library frequently with your child. Explore the shelves together. Pick out a big stack of books. As soon as you've read your way through them, go back and get more.

As your child gets older, suggest new genres. If he has read only fiction, suggest nonfiction. If she is stuck on Old World romances, suggest an Old West biography.

Reading Lists Obtain a suggested reading list for your child's age group. Most school librarians will have one or more such lists. Magazines such as *Parent* print lists of recommended and award-winning titles. Pick up a book or two from this list each time you visit the library.

Reference Tools As your child gets older, spend more time in the library—perhaps an entire evening every couple of weeks. If your child has homework to do, let her do it there with dozens of reference books at her disposal. If he simply wants to read while *you* do some research, that's OK. The point is, both parent and child are in the library rather than plunked down in front of the TV.

Your child may have a research project to do. Encourage him to take on the project as a challenge to see how much he can learn and how interesting he can make the topic, not how little he can get by with for a passing grade.

Show your child how to use the library's reference materials. Don't overlook the librarian as a resource. Teach your child how to ask questions of a librarian and to say "thank you" for the assistance. Take on some minor research projects together—perhaps related to your child's pet, a home-repair project, or an upcoming family vacation. Enjoy exploring and researching together.

Source of Resources   Much of what your child will need to know fifty years from now hasn't been discovered yet. The best you and your child's teachers can hope for is this: to teach your child basic skills and to teach your child *how* to learn. A library is one place in our society geared for helping us learn how to learn.

8 • Discuss Current Events

Talk about the news with your child.

School lessons and news programs are excellent vehicles for presenting facts, concepts, and principles. It is only as your child overlays that information with values, however, that she will know what to think about, how to feel about, or how to respond to the information she has been given. The expression of values and opinions is part of *your* role as an aware and concerned parent.

In discussing the news with your child, you are modeling behaviors closely associated with learning and schooling:

- drawing a strong link between school subjects and real-life applications.

- displaying curiosity in the world around you.

- placing a high value on discussion and an exchange of opinions.

Confront Fears   News reports about natural catastrophes, wars, civil unrest, or crime can instill a deep-seated sense of distrust or fear in a child. Educational research studies show that children who are exposed to great amounts of television violence (either as news or as entertainment) tend to rate their neighborhoods and cities as being much more violent than they actually are.

Talk about the issues underlying the conflict. Show your child on a map where conflicts or catastrophes have occurred. Dispel your child's fears as best you can. If you live in a high-crime area, talk to your child about safety.

Decipher Issues   Especially during election years, discuss political issues with your child. Talk about possible causes and effects, and give your opinions and reasons about why certain programs do not, might not, may, or do work.

Talk About Solutions   As much as possible, keep your conversations about the news positive and forward-looking. Help your child develop problem-solving and conflict-resolution skills.

Don't limit yourself to national or international news. Talk about happenings in your hometown. Build a sense of responsibility in your child—a sense of civic pride that can one day demonstrate itself through volunteer activities or public service.

Above all, draw out your child's opinions and feelings. Children have a pretty good understanding of what is right, just, and fair. Hear out her opinions. Explore his conclusions. Applaud her attempts at reason and logic.

9 • Teach Your Child How to Outline Ideas

A skill critical to school success is being able to make an outline. An outline helps a child separate important ideas from ones of less importance.

    I. Outlines are the bases of nearly all curriculum materials.
       A. Lectures and classroom presentations
       B. Textbooks
       C. Lab and practicum assignments
   II. Outlines can help your child organize information.
       A. In making sense of lecture notes
       B. In preparing written assignments
       C. In organizing information to prepare for a test
 III. Outlines are time-savers.
       A. A quick means of review before a test
       B. A way of categorizing information for use later
 IV. Outlines are based on the ability to differentiate between major and minor ideas.

Major Points   To create an outline, a child needs to isolate the major points of a talk, paper, or chapter. Ask your child after you both hear a presentation, a monologue from someone, or a documentary, "What were the main ideas?"

After your child has been able to identify two or three major ideas, ask, "What other ideas were a part of that major idea?" Or "What reasons did the person give for that idea?" Or "What evidence did the person provide in support of that idea?"

Show your child how to outline ideas on paper. You may want to use a method like that illustrated previously. Or you may want to label ideas as major and minor.

10 • Turn Off the TV

Limit the amount of hours your child watches television. Although it's unrealistic to suggest that your child *never* watch TV, you may want to try a family "TV OFF" week. Talk, exercise, go out, or play together as a family instead.

You may want to develop a voucher system—ten hours of TV viewing a week *after* homework is completed and chores are done.

Provide Alternatives   Channel your child's attention and time toward the following alternatives to TV viewing:

- Reading

- Playing games

- Working puzzles

- Participating in physical activities and sports

- Enacting stories that the child makes up

- Pursuing hobbies

- Practicing a musical instrument

Guide Your Child's Viewing Be your child's
first and foremost "TV guide."

Eliminate programs that are based on violence or that
depict sexual stereotypes or occult symbols. Turn off the
soap operas (both daytime and prime time) and programs
with heavy sexual connotations and jokes.

Choose videos over commercial television, thus elimi-
nating the barrage of commercials that tend to create an
"I wanna" syndrome.

Let your child watch programs that present child-ori-
ented dramas or reinforce learning skills. Some of these
programs may draw conclusions or make value judgments
that differ from those you are attempting to teach; whenever possible, watch programs with your child. Ask her
about the programs she watches, and discuss value-re-
lated issues.

Steer your child toward programs about nature, exotic
animals, the earth's environment, and space.

Laugh with your child at true-life and true-to-life com-
edy programs.

Children learn from all television programs, not only
those labeled "educational." Ask yourself, Do I really want
my child learning the lesson being taught by this program? If you suspect the answer is no, change channels or
turn off the tube.

11 • Discuss Movies, Concerts, and Books

Don't *send* your child to a movie or a concert. Go along.

Don't suggest that your child read a book and report on it to you. Read the same book and discuss it with him.

Children become excited about learning when adults they love participate in the learning process with them and then use shared experiences as a springboard for conversations.

Shared Viewing Choose events that both you and your child find intriguing. Most cities offer theatrical productions and concerts geared toward young audiences. If your child is learning to play a band or orchestra instrument, he will likely be interested in attending a grown-up symphony concert, too! Don't discount ballet and opera. Children usually find the dance maneuvers and vocal calisthentics interesting.

Don't overexplain the performance before it begins. You may want to give your child some general guidelines about what to expect or what will be involved in the production, but don't give away the punch line or tell the whole story. (Clue your child in to when to applaud.)

Sit between children whenever possible, and insist that respect be shown to the performers. Take opera glasses or binoculars if you have them. Children enjoy a close-up view of performers.

After the performance, go out for a treat, and talk about what you have seen. Don't grill your child, or ask, "What did you learn from this?" Rather, ask,

- "What was your favorite part?"

- "How did you feel when _____ ?"

- "How do you compare this with _____ [name a prior event]?"

Listen closely to what your child says, and be willing to offer your own opinions and ideas. Show enthusiasm for the performance and the event. Even if the performance wasn't top-notch, applaud all aspects that you can. Your goal is to encourage a curious spirit.

By all means, feel free to leave a performance during an intermission or between numbers. It's better to enjoy half a concert together than to remember only that you endured the last twenty minutes.

Shared Reading   Especially as your child enters teen years, freely share magazine articles or books that you have found insightful, inspiring, or instructive. Topics can range widely—from a favorite devotional to a novel to a brochure on sexually transmitted diseases.

Ask your child to return the item to you after she has read it (which keeps you from asking repeatedly whether she *has* read it). Ask, "What do you think? Did you have any questions?" Share some of your questions or concerns, and volunteer your opinions *after* your child has expressed hers.

In sharing learning experiences and discussing them, you are reinforcing the very process of school itself, which is a place for learning information and talking about it. You are giving your child a foundation of information, experiences, and insights on which to build his opinions about life. And you are exposing your child to his culture as a full-fledged participant.

12 • Encourage Your Child to Participate in Competitive Activities

Children can learn a great deal through guided competition—competitive activities that are bathed in individual support and couched in terms of team play.

Team Play Activities that involve team identification and yet allow for competitive individual effort include the following:

- Most team sports, such as softball, baseball, soccer, football, and water polo

- Team competition with individual performances, such as tennis or swimming

- Debate and other speech team events

- Band, orchestra, or other performance group competitions against groups from other schools

In each example, the individual competes as part of a larger group. She receives emotional support and can be cheered enthusiastically as part of a team. Subpar individual performances are frequently compensated by success-ful performances from other team members.

Through such competition, children learn how to win and lose, how to support other team members, and how to take on a position within a group. They develop personal confidence and skills while maximizing their chances for and feelings of success.

Individual Competition   Individual competition —such as submitting a painting to an art exhibit, raising an animal for the fair, or participating in an individual athletic event—also has benefits. It allows a child to stretch his abilities and to explore his potential. It also forces a child, in a more direct and sometimes more pain-ful way, to come to grips with the sadness of failure or the pride of success. If your child chooses to compete in one-on-one events, talk to him about winning, losing, and plac-ing. Support your child, and express love and appreciation for him no matter where he finishes. Point out that life has a mixture of successes and failures, and that nobody wins or loses *all* the time.

Freedom to Compete   Encouraging your child to participate in competitive activities is not the same as forc-ing your child to compete. If your child doesn't want to play a certain sport or try out for a certain team, don't force the issue. Your child may be a fan rather than a player, and fans are sometimes as competitive as players!

13 • Encourage Your Child to Participate in Cooperative Activities

Competition should always be balanced by cooperation. Don't let your child become involved exclusively in competitive events or enter all relationships with a competitive attitude. He'll miss out on some of life's most fundamental lessons.

Cooperative Play From the earliest ages, encourage your child to play cooperatively with others. Much of fantasy play—in which children make up stories and improvise roles, props, and scenes—can and should be cooperative. Playing house, store, school, office, and town should be cooperative activities. Purchase toys and games that promote cooperation. If your child is interested in board or card games, suggest that she play at least half of the matches in a cooperative way with a partner.

Clubs Encourage your child to participate in clubs with open membership, ones that do not have tryouts or exclusive membership but are open to all who meet non-discriminatory criteria.

Inclusive Activities Some schools open activities such as choir, dance classes, or theatrical performances to all students who are interested. Although a student may not be the "star," he is usually given a role to play, such as painting scenery or managing the music library. Children are allowed to participate solely on the basis of desire rather than skill. Encourage your child to try some of these activities.

The lessons learned from cooperative groups are invaluable:

- Each person has a role to fill in a group.

- Working together accomplishes more than working separately.

- Group dynamics compensate for individual weaknesses or lack of skill.

- Cooperating can be more fun than competing.

- Roles shift from time to time, place to place, and group to group.

The child who learns cooperative behavior at home is far more skilled at working on small group projects at school and learns far more from them.

14 • Teach Your Child How to Read a Textbook

Teachers teach children how to read words and stories. Very few teachers, however, teach children how to read their textbooks to get the most out of them.

Children learn to read from storybooks where the plot of the story is sequential, chronological, consequential. Textbooks, by contrast, are organized in a topical fashion. They are more like encyclopedias than novels.

Getting the Overall Picture Point out to your child that her textbook has probably been written from an outline. In fact, you may want to suggest that she outline the textbook as a way of illustrating that point to herself. Headlines are the key—division, chapter, and subhead. Before your child begins to read a textbook, help her see the chapter she is reading in the context of the whole subject. As she reads one section of a chapter, help her see it in the context of the whole chapter.

Encourage your child to thumb all the way through a textbook—to get a feel for the whole of the subject and the book before he begins reading page one.

One of the best ways to illustrate the learning techniques required by textbooks is to refer to a telescope, a microscope, or the zoom lens of a camera. From time to time, it's helpful to zoom in on details and then zoom out to see the big picture. Show your child that information is related—principles build on principles, facts tend to cluster together, and concepts are related.

The End of the Chapter Many textbooks have study questions, exercises, summaries, or role-playing activities at the end of a chapter. Teach your child to look at these items *before* she begins reading. They are the clues about what the textbook editor and probably your child's teacher consider the most important points in the material. By having these questions and exercises in mind before she reads, she'll learn more from the lesson as she goes along.

In teaching your child how to read a textbook, you are also giving him a head start on how to study for a test. He'll begin to organize information and store it in memory in a way that will make test preparation easier.

15 • Teach Your Child How to Ask the Right Questions

As the old adage goes, "To get the right answers, you need to ask the right questions."

Boldness to Ask Encourage your child to ask questions politely but boldly and directly. A child's honest questions are always worthy of being addressed.

Set an example by being bold in asking questions. Don't be too embarrassed to pull over and ask directions if you get lost. You'll be setting an example for your child to follow when he gets "lost" in math class!

Ask about something that seems obvious to everyone else. If you genuinely don't know what's going on or what everyone else is talking about in a conversation, ask! You'll be setting an example for your child to follow when he finds himself adrift in a class discussion.

Children frequently stop asking questions because others make fun of them for asking. Point out to your child that other children usually make fun to hide their own ignorance of a topic. One of the easiest ways to turn the tables is for your child to ask those who are snickering, "I'm sorry I don't know the answer. But since you apparently do, would you be so kind as to tell me?"

Why and How? Much of school material is concerned with who, what, when, and where information. But the important questions for the application of information —and the questions that truly can help a child prepare for the rest of life—are *why* and *how*.

You can tie a person in knots, of course, by asking *why*. If you suspect that your child is asking *why* to manipulate you, ask, "Why are you curious about this?" If a child has a legitimate interest or concern, he'll be able to state the reason he wants to know *why*. Address those questions as best you can.

Why did this happen? Why did he take that action? Why did he say what he said? Why didn't he do something else? All of these questions are aimed at life's "motivating forces."

How did it work? How was it invented? How did she accomplish that? How did she know to do what she did? Such questions are directly related to the practical side of life—making things happen, making things work.

Point Your Child to Answers You need not have all the answers. In fact, you can't have all the answers, so don't try to. Some questions don't have an answer. Be honest with your child about that.

Many of your child's questions can be answered by reference books or experts. Point your child to the vast resources of your local library. Make "let's look it up" a common phrase in your home.

Question Protocol   When your child asks a question, do your best to answer it immediately. If you are unable to take the time for an answer, ask her to bring it up again when you can give it your full attention.

If your child asks a tough personal question, you can always say, "I'd rather not discuss that with you at this time. I'd rather wait until you're older." The answer legitimizes the question but gives you time to collect your thoughts.

Insist that your child "hear out" answers and that he listen to an answer fully before interrupting with another question.

Let your child know that questioning is a two-way street. You should feel free to ask her questions just as she asks them of you.

16 • Enlist Your Child's Help in Planning Events

Are you planning a party?

Have you been asked to chair a committee?

Are you working on a community project?

Is Thanksgiving dinner at your house this year?

Ask your child to help you with the planning and the doing!

Parties and Festive Meals Social events and holiday celebrations—for your child, for your family, or for yourself—can become activities in which to involve children at several stages.

Organization Let your child help you plan activities, menus, guest lists, and entertainment. She'll learn about how to organize ideas and break a large project down into doable pieces.

Timelines Let your child help you plan a timeline for the event—setting dates for when invitations need to be mailed, when the cake needs to be ordered, when the flowers need to be delivered. He will gain a sense of how to factor time into an activity and learn the value of planning ahead.

Creative design   Let your child help you make or choose decorations, place mats, invitations, table decorations, and so forth. Talk to her about design and your reasons for putting certain things together. Look for your child's sparks of creativity.

Budgeting and shopping   Let your child see how you budget for the event, and take him along when you shop. Make it something of a game to stay well within your budget. Your child will have a real-life math exercise and will learn about making choices and compromises as part of making and living within a budget.

Some children tend to grow up thinking that holiday events and parties just "happen." By being involved in the process, your child will gain insights into how some school subjects relate to real life, such as math and art. Perhaps more important, she'll learn about what it means to make a plan and execute it.

Community, Church, and Club Activities

Occasionally solicit your child's help in your community service. It may be setting up chairs for the church potluck dinner. It may be gathering aluminum cans to pay for a club event or community gift. Such activities teach your child the importance of service and group effort. They show your child that his group projects at school have a real-life counterpart.

17 • Build a Home Reference Library

Set aside part of your budget for the purchase of quality reference materials of benefit to your entire family.

A Dictionary If your child is young, you may want to purchase a children's dictionary with lots of pictures in it. Be sure to have a standard dictionary even if you don't have a children's dictionary. Your child will always need to be able to look up the spellings and meanings of words. Show him how to use a dictionary—including how to interpret the pronunciation and accent marks.

You may also want to teach your child to use a dictionary as a means of expanding her vocabulary. If she opens a dictionary at random and learns just one new word a day, her vocabulary will grow geometrically, and she'll have an increasing appreciation for words. Encourage her to use a new word in at least three or four sentences the same day she learns its definition and pronunciation.

An Atlas Treat your child to the world! Atlases include much more information than just maps. Cultural geography is a field your child will probably find exciting.

A Thesaurus As your child learns to write, show him how to use a thesaurus to add variety to his writing and to expand his vocabulary.

Encyclopedia If at all possible, invest in an encyclopedia, and don't let it gather dust. Use it often to answer questions (even if you're the one raising the question!).

Classic Literature Invest in some classic series—books that your child will enjoy reading and rereading. Include the Bible.

Art Books You may not be able to take your child to the Louvre or the New York Metropolitan Museum, but you can expose her to some of the great masterpieces of the world by means of books.

How-To Books   Children's cookbooks, how-it-works books, and craft and activity books help your child learn how to apply science, art, and math to real life.

Book Gift Giving Include books on your gift list for birthdays, Christmas, Hanukkah, graduations, and other special days. You may want to give yourselves a major reference book as a family gift at Christmas.

18 • Attend Church School

Religion is a *part* of your culture. It may, indeed, *be* your culture. Church school teaches and reinforces the customs, traditions, and basic concepts of faith that you hold to be important as a family. It allows your child to associate with others who hold those traditions and concepts to be vital for life. And it helps your child learn by doing in matters of faith and worship.

Meaningful Concepts Your child attends school on a mandatory basis five days a week—to learn the facts and figures you hold to be important for your child to become a functional adult. You might want to make attending church school at least once a week a mandatory activity. After all, it exposes your child to concepts and principles that make all of life meaningful as well as provide a glimpse into the life to come! Consider it a time for your child to be educated to become a fully functional citizen of heaven.

If your church school only entertains children rather than teaches them the principles and literature of your faith—or if it excludes children from the full life of the church—find a new parish, group, or synagogue in which to become involved as a family.

Other Church Activities If your church has a children's choir, consider involving your child in that program. She will learn about music, ceremony, tradition, and group dynamics. Also consider letting your child serve in an acolyte or altar-assistant position. Take him to church events—weddings, baptisms, confirmations, Ash Wednesday services, Christmas pageants, Passover meals —whatever is appropriate and central to your faith. Let your child be a participant whenever possible, not merely an observer. Children learn by *doing,* and in no arena is that more essential than in worship.

Reinforcing School Subjects Help your child draw parallels between her church school lessons and regular school subjects. Look for crossovers in history, literature, art, music, science, and cross-cultural studies. Point out to her the value of reading and studying the Scriptures for herself. Help her learn how to use a concordance to find passages of the Bible related to her problems or questions.

19 • Let Your Child Become a Gardener

Children learn by tending a garden or by growing a crop —even if it's only bean sprouts, a potato plant, or an avocado seedling.

Flowers or Veggies? Let your child choose what he'd like to grow. Point out plants that have a short germination period and a short time between germination and fruit bearing. If he is allowed to make the decision, he'll be more motivated to do the work.

All Aspects of Gardening Let your child map out her area of turf, prepare the soil, plant the seeds, water, weed, prune or train, harvest, and clear the ground for the next cycle. Let her research what varieties of plants and flowers grow best in your climate and type of soil (a good reading exercise or research project). Let her measure out the distance between types of plants or between seeds (a good math exercise). Show your child how to keep track of dates and yields. Teach her how to weigh produce or count blooms from a seed (again, a good math exercise). Encourage your child to do a research project related to the bugs or plant diseases that might attack her crop as well as possible remedies.

Size   Perhaps the most discouraging aspect of gardening to a child—apart from long germination periods—is having too much garden. Keep his garden plot down to a child-management size. It may be a half-barrel garden on the patio or deck, a row of four-inch herb pots in a kitchen garden window, or a small cactus garden on a window sill. A lot of zucchini, carrots, radishes, corn, and beans can be grown in a plot of earth only eight feet by six feet.

The Harvest   Use harvest time to teach your child the value of sharing and preserving. Some of the flowers might be taken to a friend who is ill or in a nursing home. Some of the flowers might be pressed and turned into a lasting craft project. Vegetables can be shared with neighbors. New recipes can be tried. Some of the vegetables might be frozen or canned for later use. Be innovative and creative. Just as you let your child decide what to grow, let her take the lead in deciding what to do with the harvest.

Other Ways to Enhance Learning   Your child might enjoy taking photographs of his garden project at each stage of the process. He might enjoy making tracings of plant leaves or building a collection of seeds. He might enjoy making paintings or drawings of bouquets created from the flowers he has grown. He might create his own gardening baskets or stitch his own knee pads. Encourage your child to approach it as a creative project and to continually search for new gardening methods.

Bringing Science Alive A garden brings the entire subject of science alive for a child. It teaches valuable lessons about life's cycles. It encourages your child to become a tender of the earth and a good steward of all living things.

20 • Expose Your Child to Computers

Our children live in the computer age. The computer is becoming the primary tool of learning, working, producing, communicating, and record keeping. Your child doesn't need to know how a computer works as much as how to work it. (It's a little like the difference between knowing how a car works and knowing how to drive it.)

More than Games Computer games have their place. They're a fine way of helping a child become familiar with a keyboard, enhance eye-hand coordination, discover through experience some of the ways in which a computer program might "layer" information, and gain an interest in learning more about computers—all while having fun. You are wise, however, to limit your child's play with computers and to channel some of that computer time into other ways of learning.

Many excellent computer programs help your child acquire reading, spelling, math, and geography skills. Other programs allow your child to experiment with elements of design and the actual creation of computer programs. You may want to invest in quiz-style programs that test your child's knowledge (against grade level).

The primary advantage of the computer in all these

subject areas, of course, is motivation. Children *like* using computers and exerting control over a machine as part of the learning process. Therefore, they are likely to spend more time studying with computers than with some other media.

Benefits and Limitations   At the heart of computer-program logic are three primary functions.

Yes-no answers   Computers work in a yes-no, on-off manner. They are only as good as the data fed into them and the options provided for them. Computers are a great way to reinforce the learning of specific discrete data. Press the right answer and get a new screen. Press the wrong answer and get a reprimand. Skills such as math, spelling, history, science principles, and geography are good ones for computerized grilling and drilling.

Point out to your child, however, that all of life isn't a yes-no, black-white proposition. Encourage your child to break away from the computer to explore experiences and to engage in conversations that have no set patterns or pat answers.

Storing and accessing information   Work with your child as she works a computer. Suggest ways in which she might store information for later use. Decide which items should be kept in long-term (hard drive) memory and which ones can be kept in short-term access (disks, CDs, or tapes).

Computing and processing data   A computer functions best when it is asked to collate information in new and unusual ways. Give your child the freedom to experiment with a computer—truly to explore all that it is capable of doing.

Computer Literacy   How can you help your child become computer literate? If his school doesn't offer access to, and training in, computers, find a computer store or camp that does. Investigate computer usage at the public library. Consider investing in a computer for your home use (if you don't already have one). Explore programs geared for the age level of your child.

In helping your child master computers, you are helping him master his future, and you may be keeping him from being mastered by systems and machines.

21 • Discuss Your Child's Homework

Show an interest in the work that your child brings home from school—both what has been done and what is still undone.

Here are four questions to ask your child about homework:

1. "Do you have homework to do tonight?"
2. "What kind of homework do you have?"
3. "How long do you think it will take you to do your homework?"
4. "Do you need any reference materials or help with your homework?"

Answers to these questions will help you plan your family's evening. You may need to stop by the library. You'll also be able to compare answers to questions two and three to see if your child is being reasonable about the time he is planning to invest in getting his homework finished. Some children think that they can finish their homework in a matter of minutes.

Insist that your child complete her homework *before* watching television or engaging in any recreational activities (apart from team sports that might hold practice sessions immediately after school).

Also insist that he work without the distractions of radio, stereo, or television. Don't buy the argument that he can concentrate better if there's noise in the background. Research shows that students who make noise a part of study tend to develop shorter attention spans.

To insist on quiet, of course, you need to create a generally quiet atmosphere in your home or provide a place where your child can go to do homework without distractions.

Helping Out   If your child requests your assistance with homework, help as best you can without doing the homework for her. Discuss concepts or a topic on which she is assigned to write an essay or do a research project. You might steer her toward appropriate reference materials or experts to interview. You might help your child by going over her homework after she has completed it and suggesting that she may want to rework a problem or check the spelling of a word.

Long-Term Assignments   Many students have difficulty pacing themselves to complete major projects that are due several weeks after they are assigned. An additional question to ask an older child periodically is this: "Has your teacher given you any term papers or big projects to do?" If so, suggest to your child that you sit down together and map out a plan for getting that project finished. Schedule a couple of sessions at the library. Set interim "due dates" for parts of the project—research, outline, draft, final draft.

Good Work   Post good work and test scores where all in the family can learn about and applaud the effort— perhaps on the refrigerator door. Ask your child if you can read his finished term papers. You'll gain valuable insights into your child's progress, and he'll appreciate knowing that you value and encourage his best efforts.

Questionable Assignments Use homework assignments as an opportunity to thumb through your child's textbooks. You'll get an idea of what she is studying and is being taught. If you don't like something you read or see, remediate that assignment. You may want to suggest an "op-ed" approach to the essay—one that presents the opposing editorial view. You may want to talk over the assignment with your child and share with her why you are concerned or troubled. You may want to discuss some of the assignments with your child's teacher or principal or bring textbook issues to the attention of other parents.

Public schools in our nation are organized on a district level so that parents in each region of the country can have a say in what their children are being taught. There is no national or state curriculum. Furthermore, there are many ways, means, and teaching methods to help students score satisfactory results on state competency exams. If you and other parents in your area are concerned about the textbooks and materials from which your children are being taught, say so!

22 • Travel with Your Child

Travel is one of the most educationally stimulating gifts you can ever give your child. The trip need not be extensive or expensive. In fact, you may want to engage in a series of one-day excursions in your city or town.

The Zoo Read the information posted at each cage, pen, or display.

Walking Tours Many cities have cultural walking tours through their downtown, waterfront, or newly renovated historic districts.

Factories and Farms Explore the possibility of touring a nearby factory or farm.

Field Trips Companies, service agencies, and tourist sites frequently have special rates for schools or for children. You may want to start a "Saturday Field Trip" club with your child and some of his friends to take advantage of group rates to monuments or parks that are within a couple of hours driving time.

Galleries and Monuments   Children love
hands-on museums—ones with levers to pull, buttons to push, and experiments to perform. They enjoy galleries and museums with exhibits geared toward their own experience. Children are intrigued with displays of dinosaur bones. They are fascinated by planetarium programs. They enjoy real-life models that they can walk through, sit in, or walk under.

Family Vacations   If you're planning a vacation
away from your city, let your child help with the research. Send for brochures that describe key attractions in the area where you are going. Mix pure entertainment with cultural or instructional experiences. Make attending a concert, play, reenactment, slide presentation, or drive through a Civil War battlefield a time for talking about history, cultural trends, or scientific discoveries. Explore foods "native" to a region.

Some of the greatest lessons of travel, of course, are involved with travel itself—how to plan an itinerary, how to be flexible when unforeseen circumstances arise, how to budget a trip, how to make wise souvenir purchases, how to tip a bellcap and be a good hotel guest, how to ride a trolley car or subway, how to read a map, how to pack a suitcase.

If you are able to travel to a foreign nation, your child will learn a new currency, many new customs, and perhaps even a new language. Teach your child to be a kind, curious, and adaptable traveler. Those lessons translate into all circumstances of life.

23 • Write to Pen Pals

Encourage your child to have a pen pal—or several—in another nation or region of the country.

- Enlarge your child's vision of the world. A child benefits from seeing that the world is a place filled with children, many of whom have similar interests, most of whom have differences of culture, and some of whom are facing major challenges in their lives.

- Stimulate your child's interest in geography, world news, cross-cultural studies, languages, and world history.

- Help your child develop writing skills. Most children sincerely want their letters to reflect good grammar and spelling.

Encourage your child to write for freebies or to purchase inexpensive items, such as postcards or patches, to send to a pen pal. This different type of letter writing—letters more of the business variety—will give your child an added opportunity to work on penmanship, composition, and spelling.

Include your child's pen pal(s) in times of prayer for

the nations of the world. Exchange photographs. Research the nation in which your child's pen pal lives. Find out about the weather, time zone, geography, language, culture, and natural resources.

Other Types of Pen Pals Your child may want to write to a soldier who is stationed overseas or to a missionary (or child of a missionary) that you support as a family or church or to a prisoner. Urge your child to write words of encouragement or look up Scriptures to share to give hope and build faith.

Letters of One's Own Children love to receive mail addressed to them. Mail call is even more exciting when the letters are from a pen pal from a faraway place. Your child may want to collect the stamps from a pen pal's letters or to make a pen pal scrapbook.

24 • Eat Out with Your Child

Don't leave your child at home with a baby-sitter every time you go out to eat. Share dining experiences with her. Be innovative. Try new foods. Don't limit yourself to fast-food restaurants. Occasionally splurge at a place that calls upon her best manners.

Choices Dining out involves choices. In school terms, making choices is called making decisions. Tell your child in advance what parameters you are placing on his choices—for example, price of entree, type of beverage, and permission for dessert. Then allow your child freedom to make choices.

If you question whether your child will enjoy certain spices, condiments, sauces, or dressings, ask for them to be served on the side. That way your child can experiment, and if she doesn't enjoy the new taste sensation, she'll still have basic food to eat and enjoy.

If you are served a dish with an unusual flavor, approach it a little like a science project—try to discern what spices or herbs have been used. See who can come the closest to identifying the unusual tang or aroma.

Culture Dining out can introduce your child to a new culture. If the waiters or waitresses are from another culture or nation, take some time to talk to them and ask them about their homeland. Even if you are eating in an all-American Mom-and-Pop cafe, engage waiters and waitresses in conversation, especially if you're eating at a slow time, which, by the way, is always a good idea when dining out with children. Restaurant personnel usually know an area well, and they can provide you with invaluable tips if you are traveling.

Social Graces At a fine restaurant, you can teach your child social graces that will come in handy all his life. He'll learn how to conduct himself at the table, how to use various pieces of cutlery and glassware, how to order, and how to deal with the bill and tip.

Many fine restaurants include live music. Teach your child how to acknowledge the music, how to make musical requests, and how to acknowledge good performance.

Indoor Adventure Approach dining out as a learning adventure. Try new restaurants. You may want to let your child make the decision sometimes. Take your time and make the experience relaxed and fun. Even if the setting is elegant, the conversation can be lively. Tell jokes. Recall family stories. Laugh. Your child will hold these classes in dining out as pleasant memories and useful instruction for life.

25 • Attend Cultural Events with Your Child

Make it a point to take your child to cultural events.

A Symphony Concert Arrive early enough to read the program notes about the music that is going to be played. Talk to your child about the instruments in the orchestra. Let your child know when to applaud. Take along opera glasses or binoculars so your child can get a close-up view.

A Play or Musical Many old Broadway-style musicals have plots that a child can follow and enjoy, such as *Peter Pan* or *Meet Me in St. Louis.* He'll likely be awed by the scenery, costumes, and lighting effects. Bible-based pageants are staged across the nation, especially during holidays and the summer months. Shakespearean productions are common summer theater fare.

A Ballet *The Nutcracker* plays in many cities during the December holiday season. *Cinderella* is another enjoyable ballet for children.

An Opera Your child—age ten or older—may find opera to her liking. Since most operas are sung in a language other than English, consider attending a production that has the words summarized in English in an overhead projection manner that's unobtrusive, yet readily viewed.

Whenever possible, do advance research before attending an opera or a Shakespearean play to give children clues about the plot and characters.

An Ice Show Ice Capades and Ice Follies programs are a child's delight. Wonderfully staged, they trigger a child's imagination and provide an unusual entertainment experience.

A Professional Sporting Event Take your child to watch baseball, football, tennis, ice hockey, basketball, or soccer. Let your child experience the thrill of competition at its highest level of skill. Of course, if you are a fan of one of the teams, the event will be all the more exciting.

An Animal Show It may be a circus, a rodeo, a state fair competition, an equestrian competition, a race, or a major animal show (such as a dog show or other type of pet show).

Special Exhibits From time to time, communities host special exhibits: flower shows, automobile shows, boat shows, home shows, and toy shows. Take your child to at least one such event in his life. He'll be amazed at the variety of products or species he sees.

Culture Awareness   Are all of these *cultural* events? Absolutely! After the event, talk about what you have experienced with your child. Relate it to school in as casual a way as possible. What subjects in school are a part of the first-rate performance you've seen—such as the historical period in which a play or an opera is based, the need for math in the construction of sets (as well as the composing of music), the relationship between a composer or an author and his culture? Is a baseball diamond truly a diamond? What division and addition skills are represented by a football field and football's scoring system? What geometry angles are involved in a rapid-fire game of doubles tennis?

Also explore with your child the school-related skills required by the performers, such as memorization, concentration, experimentation, and discipline.

26 • Explore Nature with Your Child

Go on an overnight camp out. Or if camping isn't a favorite activity, take an occasional nature walk with your child. The walk may even be one around your neighborhood or in a city park.

Invest in a pair of binoculars for your child before you go. Watch for birds and animals. You may want to take a camera with you so you can capture some of these creatures on film for later identification or study.

Collect twigs, leaves, rocks, shells, fossils, or seeds. Make certain that you know exactly what you are touching (such as poison ivy or poison oak). Don't eat any berries or mushrooms that you pick until you are absolutely —repeat, absolutely—certain that what you have gathered is safe to eat.

Collections Encourage your child to build a nature collection. Seeds. Shells. Rocks. Pressed flowers. Label your child's findings by species, date, and place. Encourage your child to read about what you have seen or brought home. You'll be reinforcing basic science studies without pain!

Wilderness Skills   Reading a compass, charting a course, reading a map, determining the time of day, learning safety procedures—all these skills apply math, geography, and science lessons.

Creative Activities   Take along a sketch pad or notebook. If your child enjoys art, give her time to sketch or paint a scene. Perhaps you'll want to stop for a few minutes to let everyone in your party write in a journal.

Wounded Animals   Before caring for orphaned or injured animals and birds, make certain that they are not likely to be carriers of rabies, fleas, or ticks, or that they aren't capable of causing a serious bite. Nurturing a nest of abandoned birds or a litter of orphaned kittens can be a wonderful learning opportunity for your child.

Farms and Petting Zoos   If you live in a city, take your child to the country occasionally. Visit a farm. Go to a petting zoo. Let your child see animals up close.

Camps and Ranch Vacations   Send your child to a camp that has outdoor wilderness-style activities— swimming, fishing, canoeing, horseback riding, and so forth.

Scouting   Your child can explore nature by taking part in a scouting program (such as Boy Scouts, Girl Scouts, Camp Fire, Royal Rangers, and so forth).

Enjoy the Seasons   Revisit the same trail or path four times in a year—once a season. Point out to your child the differences in the area from season to season. You may want to make a log of each experience.

A child learns to value what you value. If you value clean air, clean water, and unspoiled wilderness areas and beaches, your child will value them, too. If you advocate good stewardship of the earth, your child will want to be a good steward.

27 • Consult Maps

Have you just heard about a natural catastrophe or a war in a faraway place with a strange-sounding name?

Does your child have an assignment about eighteenth-century Europe?

Is your child studying the natural resources and economies of South American nations?

Bring out the maps! Up-to-date maps can help your entire family make a little more sense of the world.

Topical relief maps and three-dimensional "model" maps are especially intriguing to children. Point out cities to your child as you view such maps and ask, "Why do you think a city was built there?"

Cultural maps and economic maps—ones that divide areas of the world according to religion, language, economic average, natural resources, and so on—offer special insight into the way the world works.

You may want to purchase a national or world map to hang in your child's room as a reminder that the world is a big place and one worth exploring. Or you may want to invest in a globe. Try playing "spin the globe" with your child. As you spin it, put your finger down on one spot, and ask the other person to name the country in which you have landed.

Historical Maps Children are frequently amazed to discover that the view of the world hasn't always been the way it is today or that the nations in existence today haven't always been here. Compare maps over the past two hundred years.

Trip Maps Are you planning a trip? Let your child play navigator for a while each day. He can hold the map, give directions, and chart your progress. (You can always have a second map accessible to the driver.)

A New City Are you moving to a new city? Acquire a map that will be exclusively for your child's use. Let her mark it up with her favorite new places. It will give her confidence.

Make a Map Encourage your child to make up maps of his room, your house, the neighborhood, your part of town, and his school. Teaching him how to draw to scale is an exercise in math, measurement, and geometry. You might also challenge him to make up an imaginary town or island, complete with map.

28 • Take Responsibility for Your Child's Sex Education

Be your child's first teacher about sexual behavior. If you find it a difficult subject to discuss with your child, take advantage of books and videotapes on the market that can help you launch a discussion.

Perhaps the best approach a parent can take is to talk about sexual behavior as a normal and natural part of life and to intersperse comments and opinions about sex as a part of everyday conversation. Having a one-time lecture about the birds and the bees is usually more awkward for both parents and children.

Your child is interested in sexual behavior from a very early age. He may not be the least bit curious about the details of sexual intercourse, but he probably is very curious about kissing and hugging and why people hold hands.

Your child is a sexual being from the time she is born. She is capable of feeling arousal from infancy. Educational research studies have shown that children experience titillation and sexual arousal from viewing sexual behavior portrayed by adults—kissing and hugging—as early as ages four and five (a good reason to turn off soap operas in the presence of your children!). All of this to say, no age is too early for you to address the subject of sexual behavior.

Preparation for Puberty By all means, discuss menstruation with your daughter *before* its onset. Discuss puberty with your son. As much as is possible, explain to your child what is happening in the body.

Doing What School Doesn't Most schools provide instruction about the "mechanics" of sexual behavior —with a focus on anatomy and physiology. They do *not*, however, provide a value judgment about sex. If anything, schools take a neutral position, which from a child's point of view is usually interpreted as a pro stance. As a result, school does not give your child guidelines about how to think about sex, how to value sex, how to evaluate appropriate or ideal contexts for sexual behavior, or what to do with sexual urges. Those are the areas in which you need to provide instruction for your child.

- Teach your child that sexual responsibility is an issue for *both* boys and girls.

- Talk to your child about sexual abuse, and tell him explicitly what he should do if he is ever approached by someone who demands sexual favors or who continually engages in sexual conversations or harassment.

- Discuss the issue of sexually transmitted diseases with your young teen. Discuss pregnancy and the reasons for and types of birth control.

- Above all, share with your child the difference between love and sex.

29. Help Your Child Learn to Manage Money

Money management is a part of your child's education that is up to you. Schools rarely teach personal economic skills.

Managing the Allowance For most children, the beginning of earning power is an allowance. Give your child an allowance and teach her how to manage it wisely.

The old adage of "give some, save some, and spend some" is an apt one to pass along. Teach your child how to set up a simple ledger system for recording money given, money saved, and money spent. Give your child the challenge of keeping track of her money on a weekly basis.

Once a month, ask your child to tally the columns in the ledger, figure percentages (how much of the whole was represented by each column), and make a note of where she hopes to improve her spending habits. (If your child hasn't learned how to figure percentages, figure them for her.)

Giving Money Help your child to give generously and wisely. Talk about various not-for-profit organizations, including your church or synagogue. Suggest that your child aim at giving at least 10 percent.

Saving Money Open a savings account in your child's name. He'll be delighted to see it grow and to benefit from compounded interest. Encourage him to save for something specific that is for fun—perhaps a new bicycle, skateboard, or trip—and also to save for something that is truly an investment in his future, such as college, a summer abroad program, or a special camp or course.

Spending Money Teach your child to comparison shop, to look for sales, and to recognize a true bargain when she spots one. At about age ten, let your child open a checking account. Teach her how to fill out deposit slips, balance her checking account once a month, and read bank statements. It's a real-life way for your child to learn simple economic principles.

When your child is about age sixteen, acquire a credit card in his name. Teach him the value of having good credit, and instruct him in how to use a credit card and to keep spending under control.

Talking About Money Make economics and money a part of your conversation. Tell your child where you invest your money and why. Explain why you choose some investments over others. Talk about national and international economic issues.

At tax time, explain to your child how the tax system works. If your child has a part-time job, give her the chance to fill out a tax return, even if she doesn't need to file the completed form.

Budgeting As your child begins to earn money from part-time jobs, teach him how to make a budget and how to evaluate his success in living within his means on a monthly basis. His ledger system will provide a basis for determining how much he plans to give, save, and spend. Specific categories might be designated for places to give, types of investment and savings accounts, and different categories of spending.

Above all, insist that your child learn to use money responsibly and honestly. Insist that he pay his bills—on time. Insist that he not spend beyond his income.

30 • Discuss Report Cards and School Reports

Report cards are just that—reports. Don't use them as a judgment against your child. Report card time is not a time for lectures or punishment. It *is* a time for

- praising your child for his successes.

- facing up to areas in which your child isn't doing as well as she might.

- helping your child make some mid-course corrections.

Here are three important questions to ask your child:
1. Are you pleased with your grades?
2. Where do you think you might improve?
3. What do you think you need to do to improve and do your best?

You can ask these questions even of *A* students. They usually have a feel for whether they can achieve more.

Learning Curves Most grades are comparisons. Your child may have earned a *C* because one student earned an *A* and another earned an *F*. The concern for a parent is not the grade, but whether the child is learning the information being presented in a way that will enable him to use it later. Insist that your child give school his best effort. Point out the importance you place on his ability to apply what he learns. But don't punish your child for coming home with *B*'s or *C*'s if that is his best effort. A simple rule of thumb to keep in mind is this: *Learning is what counts, not grades.*

Nonacademic Reports   Many teachers provide grades for citizenship or evaluate general behavior and perceived attitudes about learning and school. Take these marks seriously. They are just as significant as grades for academic achievement.

Most children love to learn—usually until they've had a bad schooling experience of some type. If your child is feeling negative about school, find out why.

Learning Problems   If your child enjoys school, tries hard, does her homework diligently, and still shows consistently poor marks, talk to her teacher about whether your child might have a learning disorder.

Praise and Punishment   Tell your child you are proud of his effort and his achievement. Point toward specific traits and trends that you find encouraging—for example, his improved self-discipline in doing his homework or his growing ability to ask penetrating questions or make insightful comments. Rewarding grades with money or other tangible "prizes" only encourages him to seek the prize more than the knowledge.

Do *not* punish your child for poor grades. Rather, make changes, and discuss them with your child. You may need to curtail certain activities (such as playtime or extracurricular activities), provide remediation or tutoring, or devote more of your attention to your child's study habits.

31 • Praise Your Child's Progress

Don't wait for a report card or a conversation after a parent-teacher conference to praise progress that you see in your child:

- Intellectual growth

- Study habits

- Research skills

- Perceptivity

- Writing skills

- Ability to ask valid and penetrating questions

- Ability to make insightful comments and engage in conversation

- Academic achievements

- Applications of school subjects to everyday living

Your child needs to see you as an active, daily participant in her intellectual growth—just as you are an integral part of helping her grow physically, emotionally, spiritually, and relationally.

Your comments need not be lengthy or formal. They

do need to be genuine and honest. Here are some suggestions:

- "You really are developing a string of successes in science lab, aren't you?"—perhaps after seeing a good grade on a lab exercise.

- "I enjoy conversations with you more and more"—perhaps after a particularly good interchange of ideas.

- "Your penmanship is really improving"—perhaps after looking at a pen pal letter your child has just addressed.

- "I realized last night that I no longer have to tell you to do your homework. That's a real mark of maturity I see in you."

- "You have a wonderful way of making analogies."

- "I've noticed that you hardly ever misspell words in your essays. That's a real accomplishment."

- "I'm impressed with the number of resources you used in doing this research project."

Parental praise is one of the best motivators toward greater school performance that your child will ever experience. Be generous in applauding your child's growth and successes!

Have You Told Your Child Lately

- that you are proud of his school performance?

- that you are pleased with her improvement in a particular subject area or learning skill?

- that you value his ideas and opinions?

- that you appreciate something she has taught you or is teaching you?

- that you applaud his willingness and courage to try or learn something new?

- that her education is important to you?

32 • Help Your Child Set Personal Academic Goals

Have periodic discussions with your child about what he sees as his academic or learning goals. Report card time is a good time for doing this. So is the beginning of a new school year.

Set short-range, medium-range, and long-range goals for in-school and out-of-school projects. Record these goals for future reference.

Short-Range Goals Include immediate changes the child anticipates making.

School Goals:

- Set aside an additional hour of study *before* dinner.

- Raise my English grade to a *B* from a *C*.

- Start earlier on term projects.

General Goals:

- Learn a new vocabulary word each day.

- Read my Bible ten minutes each day.

- Read one book a month that isn't a part of a school assignment.

Medium-Range Goals
Include goals for an entire school year.

School Goals:

- Raise my grade point average from a 2.5 to a 3.0.
- Try out for a school play.
- Move from the second clarinet section to the first section.
- Get an *A* in biology.

General Goals:

- Improve my typing skills.
- Get a pen pal.
- Join the science club.
- Take archery lessons.

Long-Range Goals
These may be goals related to high school (if your child is an elementary student) or college.

School Goals:

- Take a college prep course in high school.

- Score over 1200 on the SAT.

- Get accepted to the college of my choice.

General Goals:

- Read the entire Bible before graduation from high school.

- Read at least fifty of the world's greatest books by the time I'm twenty-five.

- Learn three major computer languages.

- Become fluent in French.

Be Realistic Talk over your child's goals with her. Be realistic in setting goals. Don't set too many goals—no more than five in any category. At the same time, encourage her to aim high and to give her best effort.

Ask your child how she intends to go about achieving her goals—what habits she needs to develop, what types of help she needs, what prerequisite courses or steps she may need to take. Develop a step-by-step plan, especially for medium-range and long-range goals.

Finally, set a date for reevaluating these goals. Goals should be readjusted from time to time. Priorities and interests shift. Let your child know that her goals aren't set in concrete.

33 • Subscribe to Periodicals

If textbooks are the core of the school curriculum, periodicals are likely to be at the core of "home" learning. In both environments, of course, reference books and fiction are also to be encouraged.

Newspapers Subscribe to a daily newspaper. Give your child access to it. Anticipate that your child—especially after third grade—does read the paper. Ask questions about certain articles: "Did you see the article in today's paper about _____ ?"; "What did you think about the way the game was described in the paper?"; "Wasn't that an interesting article about _____ ?" Let your child know that he can learn just by reading headlines, the first paragraph or two of an article, and captions.

Family Magazines Subscribe to at least one news magazine and one general family-interest magazine.

Children's Magazines Every child loves to receive magazines in his own name that cover areas in which he is interested. Consider these children's magazines:

- *Highlights for Children* is the classic magazine for children two to twelve years old, with stories, puzzles, and games all geared to the promotion of specific learning skills (the same company produces an excellent periodical of puzzles titled *Puzzlemania*).

- *Cricket* has stories, puzzles, poems, and contests (writing, art, photography) for children seven to fourteen years old.

- *Ladybug* presents stories, poems, songs, action games, and activities for children two to six years old.

- *American Girl* is for girls seven and older; it has stories, feature articles, and paper dolls—some of which are a takeoff on the popular American Girl book series.

- *Ranger Rick* offers science and adventure articles for both boys and girls seven and older.

Teen Magazines   Teen magazines tend to be more specialized—cars, outdoor life, or fashion. In some cases, you may want to monitor what your teen is reading. Teen magazine articles can sometimes have very explicit information about sexual behavior or portray the most bizarre fads and trends. One of the best teen magazines on the market with high moral standards is *Campus Life*.

Periodicals encourage your child to read. They introduce her to topics and genres that she may not encounter in school. Periodicals also give your child insights into how the subjects she's learning in school relate to real-life current experiences.

34 • Provide Tutoring

Don't let your child struggle year after year in a subject. In fact, don't let your child struggle more than a month or two in a subject. Get help!

The Basics Many times children pretend to know a concept or principle—sometimes they may even be convinced that they know it—and then they proceed to build on what turns out to be a very shaky or false foundation. The result is inevitably frustration and disaster.

Ask your child from time to time to show you *how* she works problems—to talk them through as she does them, step by step. Or ask your child *why* she chose a particular verb tense or grammatical construction. Discuss basic science principles with your teen.

One of the best ways of determining whether your child truly understands basic principles is to ask him to teach them to you. Another way, of course, is to consult his teacher.

As a parent, you should listen to your child read—books, passages from newspapers or magazines, signs and menus, or other materials. You should know how well your child is reading. You should review her homework and talk to her about school often enough to know what is causing her a problem and what isn't.

No Embarrassment   Everybody has difficulty learning something. That's a fact of life many people in education are just now facing. Being "smart" in one area —which may require one type of learning—doesn't mean that a child will be "smart" in another area. Different subjects sometimes require different learning skills.

- Don't take the stance that your child can do better by just trying harder. Maybe so. Maybe not. He may need some extra help in acquiring a new learning skill.

- Don't assume that your child will do better if she just listens more, does more homework, or asks more questions. She may need specialized guidance in learning *how* to learn.

Coaching   Don't look upon tutoring as a negative. It is one of the most positive things you can provide for your child. You may want to use the word *coaching*. Nearly all children understand the reason for a coach—someone to explain the rules of the game, show you how to play, and help you develop skills. A coach is nearly always a player's biggest fan, too. All in all, that's the profile of a good tutor!

Ask your child's teacher or principal for suggested tutors. Sometimes college education departments require their students to tutor children for no charge or for a nominal fee as a practicum or as part of a course. Teachers sometimes tutor during summer months. An older child in your family may be a good coach.

35 • Provide Therapy

Emotional well-being has a direct impact on a child's ability to concentrate, memorize, recall information previously learned, and express himself. In sum, how your child is *feeling* has a direct bearing on how well your child is *thinking*.

If your child has been through a traumatic experience —the loss of a beloved relative or friend, parents' divorce, a move to a new place, a major illness, or any type of sexual, physical, or emotional abuse—get help for her. A school counselor may be able to help her directly or may refer you to someone who specializes in helping children with the problem being experienced by your child. Or you may want to consult your pastor, priest, or rabbi for counsel or referral.

Problem Identification You may not be aware that your child has experienced a crisis. Watch for changes in behavior, expression of new fears, loss of appetite, avoidance behaviors (a desire to avoid a certain place, person, or situation), temper tantrums, unexpected outbursts or tears or verbal assaults, increased incidences of bed-wetting, new "clinging" behaviors (not wanting to leave your side), and so forth. These can be signals that your child is experiencing fear or anger at a very deep level.

Talk to your child. Ask if there's something wrong that he hasn't shared with you. Let him know that no matter what it is, you can handle it together. State clearly to your child that no matter what another person may have threatened, you both *will* be OK. Don't register alarm, anger, or distrust when your child expresses his pain. Hear him out. Ask for as many details as he can provide. Hold him close and comfort him. Assure him that you will take action on his behalf, and then do so.

Assumptions NOT to Make
Don't assume that a family or personal crisis didn't really affect your child. A family trauma or an abuse situation is very real to a child at many levels—and sometimes at different levels as the child grows older. He may need periodic counseling through the years as he faces new issues or relives old memories.

Don't assume that just because your child says, "I'm OK," everything really is OK. Children frequently tend to cover up their feelings to help a wounded parent, or they attempt to deny their feelings rather than face the pain.

Don't assume that your child will get over it, get through it, figure it out, recover from it, grow out of it, or forget it by herself. The greater likelihood is that the unresolved problem will continue to fester deep within your child's psyche for many years, and it may well manifest itself in violent and unexpected ways.

What does therapy provide for your child? It gives him a chance to talk, to work through anger, fears, and frustrations. It gives him tools with which to fight back at what he perceives to be injustice. Group sessions may provide peer allies.

Learning Disabilities If your child is diagnosed with a learning disability, provide therapy. A trained educator can help your child develop compensatory skills to circumvent the problem and greatly enhance your child's chances for school success. Your child may need to be given oral tests rather than written ones until these compensatory skills are developed. Your child's teacher can probably refer you to an effective learning disabilities therapist.

Speech Therapy If your child stutters, stammers, or has difficulty pronouncing certain sounds, provide speech therapy. Your child's ability to speak clearly and fluently is directly related to school success and to emotional well-being.

36 • Arrange for Lessons to Enhance Abilities

Is your child gifted in a particular area? Music? Art? Creative writing? Science? Sports? Dance? Mathematics?

Encourage Your Child's Talents and Interests Every child has at least one area of talent—something she does well and enjoys. Bear in mind that both qualities are important in identifying a true talent. The child must enjoy an area of ability as well as be good in it.

Seek Out Good Teachers Provide an outside-school teacher or coach for your child. Some of the best sources of referral are other parents.

Talk to the teachers who are recommended to you. Explain why you think that your child has a special talent. The teacher will probably ask you questions and may ask your child to talk to him or audition for him.

Several colleges and universities offer precollege courses of study for gifted students. Or the school may allow your child to enroll in a course for which she shows particular aptitude and enough prerequisite background.

One young man attended sixth grade by day and college physics classes by night. He succeeded in both places and enjoyed both experiences. He went on to earn a Ph.D. in physics while still socializing with his own age group.

Select Camps, Schools, and/or Academies
The best time to promote your child's talent may be during the summer months through attendance in a specialized camp, academy, or study program. Check out the possibilities.

Don't Provide Lessons Unilaterally
Talk to your child about special lessons. Make sure he wants to receive what you want to give. If your child has no interest in improving a skill, don't push it! His interest in that field isn't as strong as you thought.

On the other hand, just because a child is interested in improving doesn't mean that she fully understands the new level of work—practice, hours of effort, disciplined exercise, added study, or even physical pain—likely to be involved. For example, just because your child enjoys swimming and wins a few meets doesn't mean that she is willing to make all the sacrifices necessary to train for the Olympic Games.

Discuss the pros and cons of extra lessons with your child. In taking on lessons, your child will probably need to drop something else in his schedule. Your entire family may need to make some compromises and adjustments. Go into this new level of commitment to a talent with all eyes open and all hands willing.

37 • Use Good Grammar

Make good grammar a hallmark of your home.

If you question your grammar skills, take a class or buy a self-instructional book in this subject.

Let your child know that you value good grammar and a varied vocabulary. Point out that truly successful people in every walk of life use good grammar and have well-developed vocabularies. Truly successful people know how to express themselves fluently in full sentences.

When you correct your child's grammar, do so kindly, privately, with a positive reinforcer, such as adding, "I want you to be able to speak to anybody on this planet in a way that you will be understood and recognized as educated." Or "No matter what field you enter, I want you to speak as if you are a professional."

A Mutual Pact Make a pact with your child that she may correct your grammar if she hears you make a mistake, just as you correct her grammar.

Slang and Swear Words Put a cap on slang and swear words. Pull your child's conversations out of the gutter. Insist that your child learn to express himself in legitimate ways with legitimate words.

Full Sentences and Full Thoughts   Encourage your child to express herself in full sentences—to take the time to search out the words she needs and to put them together in a way that truly conveys what she means. That means you need to have patient ears as a parent. Listen to your child. Don't cut her off as she tells you a story or describes an incident.

"And Um"   Work with your child to overcome the habit of "and uh" or "and um" phrases. These can often become a habitual part of a child's speech pattern. He may not even know that he's using these phrases as often as he is.

Discipline   Good grammar and a growing vocabulary require discipline. It's easy to become lax and fall into old habits. Recognize with your child that new habits are tough to build but worth the effort.

38 • Create Environments for Conversation

Most of us learn most of what we believe through listening.

Getting Your Child to Talk   Researchers tell us that the average person gains most of his information about the world through seeing, but then those visual perceptions must be discussed, analyzed, tested, and altered. This process of turning information into opinions, beliefs, and subsequent behavior involves listening and talking.

Ask your child questions   Listen for his answers. Ask him to expand on his ideas. Ask open-ended questions, such as

- What do you think would happen if _____ ?

- What do you think is the cause of (or are the factors that led to) _____ ?

- What is your evaluation of this situation?

- If you were _____ , what would you do?

Ask for your child's opinion   Hear her out fully. If you disagree on a major principle, tell her on what points you disagree and *why*. Don't be dogmatic in voicing a general disagreement; point to specific statements with which you disagree and cite reasons for your opinion.

Engage your child in conversations   Conversations take time. They happen best in a relaxed atmosphere in which each person has an equal opportunity to participate.

Conversations are free-flowing. They have no agenda and no intended outcome other than an exchange of ideas or opinions.

Conversations allow for humorous interjections and ideological detours.

Conversations are enriching. They build relationships as well as offer a forum for an exchange of ideas and information.

Setting Up Conversations   One of the best places for conversation is the dinner table. Plan to have a family dinner at least once a week—ideally, once a day. Work together in the kitchen before the meal. Linger at the table. Clean up together. And talk!

Here are other prime times for conversations:

- After you've read a storybook to or with your child

- Over a cup of hot chocolate after you've all put on your pajamas and are seated before the fireplace or at the kitchen table

- After a bedtime story and before bedtime prayer

- In the car (with no radio playing)

- On trips to the park or to other places where you can sit and watch people or animals in relatively quiet isolation

The more you converse with your child, the easier you'll find it becomes to start a conversation, and the more rewarding these times will be. Best of all, your child will be learning to express himself. Opinions, values, and behavior-generating ideas will be forged in the process.

39 • Visit Colleges

Hold out a high ideal for your child. Anticipate that she will go on to school after high school. It may not be to a university or a college—perhaps a vocational, technical, or Bible school instead. It may be to a specialized training program or apprenticeship, an institute, an academy, or a branch of the military. Instill in your child, however, the idea that high school is the first step to higher education and better job opportunities, greater personal fulfillment, and more interesting affiliations and associations.

Start Early When should you start talking about college? Probably as soon as your child is born.

As you take family vacations, drive by college campuses in the cities and towns through which you travel. Having lunch in student unions or college cafeterias or snack bars is an excellent way of incorporating college visits into a trip.

When college field trip opportunities arise for your child, encourage him to go.

Send for college brochures when your child is a freshman in high school. Encourage her to think in terms of excelling in high school so she can have the option of going to the college of her choice.

Attend events held on college campuses—plays, concerts, athletic events, and/or special exhibits.

Include saving for college as a part of your child's savings fund.

Point to Successes When you hear of research reports, athletic successes, or prizes awarded to colleges or universities, call your child's attention to them. When a speaker is introduced and the name of a college or university is mentioned as part of the biography, make a note and remind your child of it. Your child will soon get the picture that successful people are linked to higher education.

Pursue a Goal A child who has a goal beyond high school is a child who tends to take junior-high and high-school academics more seriously. Such students try harder and learn more, even if they don't go on to college. The good news, of course, is that students who plan to go to college from the time they enter their teenage years nearly always do!

40 • Provide Good Nutrition and Sufficient Rest

Medical research is showing with increasing conviction that your child's school ability is related to her general health habits. What your child eats and how much sleep she gets on an average nightly basis directly affect her ability to "attend" to information—to perceive accurately, to process information, and to recall what has been learned.

Breakfast Make sure your child has breakfast before leaving for school. A child who hasn't eaten for twelve to sixteen hours (since dinner the night before) is a child who is going to be more concerned about lunch than arithmetic. A junk-food breakfast, however, can be just as damaging to his ability to concentrate. Provide a nutritious breakfast that includes whole grains, protein, and fruit and eliminates heavily sugared cereals and breakfast snack foods.

Nutritious Snacks and Lunches Your child *does* need an after-school snack. Children arrive home from school ravenous and energy depleted. Provide nutritious, high-energy snacks that are low in sugar. Most commercial snack foods are high in processed sugar, which leads to an immediate energy kick and a sure-to-follow energy slump. Make available an apple and a slice of cheese on a rice cracker, raw veggies and yogurt dip, or a peanut butter-and-banana sandwich. The same principle holds for school lunches. Soup and sandwiches (made with whole grains and nutrient-rich fillings) are still a good choice.

Preservatives and Additives   Attention deficit disorder (ADD) is a common diagnosis today for children once referred to as "hyper." Several ADD studies show a correlation between certain foods (resulting in food allergies) and food additives, preservatives, and sugar. The conclusion is simple: if your child is "high" on chemicals of some type, including those that may be generated by his brain, he is unable to concentrate sufficiently to focus on information or learning tasks. No concentration, no learning.

Two reference books you may want to consider in preparing meals for your child are *Feeding Your Kids Bright* by Francine Prince and Harold Prince, Ph.D., and *Cooking for Your Hyperactive Child* by June Roth. Both have lots of recipes.

Exercise   Send your child outdoors to play whenever possible. Encourage swinging, jumping rope, bike riding, skating, and playing games that involve running. The child who is on the move physically tends to be healthier, consume less junk food, and sleep better at night than the child who is inactive.

Bedtime Base your child's bedtime on breakfast time. What time in the morning does your child need to get up in order to get dressed and have breakfast before leaving for school? Backtrack from that time nine to ten hours. (Yes, children need that much sleep, and so do teenagers!) Establish a bedtime, and stick with it. Develop a rhythm in your child's life that balances sleeping, eating, and exercise.

The benefits of a healthy life rhythm are numerous for your child—an even flow of energy, a sense of well-being, a higher level of natural immunity, which results in fewer sick days (which means fewer missed days of school), and a general alertness to life.

41 • Help Your Child Find a Part-Time or Summer Job

A job for a teen tends to be one at minimum wage. Most teens quickly realize that they do not want to earn at that level for the rest of their lives. Since schooling is one of the best means for rising to a higher income bracket, a part-time or summer job is a good motivator to keep your child in school and aware of the value of schooling.

Beyond the motivational aspect, a part-time or summer job can help your child

- discover a direct relationship between what is being taught in school and what is required in the workplace.

- learn more about the value of money.

- develop discipline.

Career Insight If your child expresses an interest in a particular career, help her find a part-time job in that field or a closely related one. For example, a child interested in architecture may be able to work as an errand runner, a part-time secretary, or a clean-up worker for a construction company.

What Type of Work?   Help your child find a job that

- provides some flexibility in scheduling.

- does not pose a safety or health hazard.

- allows him to have one day a week in which he does not need to work or go to school (teens need fun and sleeping-in time, too).

If your child's health or schoolwork suffers as a result of the part-time job, insist that he stop working and concentrate on developing a healthier life-style and better study habits.

Reasons to Work   Talk about mutual expectations before your child embarks on the job search. What do you expect your child to purchase from her earnings? What are her interests? What amount of time can she expect to spend working each week without a negative impact on school or social life? Make sure the benefits of a job outweigh the possible negatives.

Family Work   You may want to hire your child to do work at home. And the money he earns should be above and beyond his allowance.

If you choose to hire your child, make sure that

- the job is a valid one. Don't make work for your child to do. He will see through that, and you may actually be training him to have less regard for work and to be less respectful of future employers.

- the job is one your child *can* do. Don't expect your child to do a job that requires adult judgment, physical coordination, or stamina.

- you pay your child a fair wage. Don't overpay or underpay her. Pay her what you'd pay an outsider for doing the same work.

- you treat your child as you would other employees. Insist on quality work, respectful behavior, and honest effort. At the same time, don't expect him to set the example or set the pace. He will not be the model employee his first day on the job.

42 • Help Your Child Find a Place to Volunteer

Volunteer work holds out many of the same learning benefits as a paying job. Through volunteering, your child or teen may have the opportunity to

- explore a possible career option, for example, in a hospital or clinic.

- learn how to work with others and to take supervision from someone other than a teacher or coach.

- be part of a team involved in problem-solving activities.

- learn more about the way our culture and society work.

- acquire new skills and information in a no-exam, practical way.

Fringe Benefits There are two added advantages to volunteer work you may not have considered.

First, volunteer work will motivate your child to learn how to help better Volunteering gives your child a sense of giving back to the community. Attending school, on the other hand, is mostly a receiving activity. In volunteer work, your child's ideas, energy, and special talents can be brought to fruition in unique and creative ways. Find a place where your child is encouraged to voice an opinion and to take an active part in the process.

A group of young teens were challenged to make their neighborhood a safer place for their younger brothers and sisters. They decided, with the approval of and a little financial assistance from an absentee landlord, to convert a vacant lot into a park. One part of the lot was devoted to a garden. Another part was seeded into a grassy area for playing games. The more the teens planned out their project and sought to implement their plans, the more they talked about their project in school. It became the content of themes for English class. The students saw a greater reason for math class. They engaged in livelier discussions in social studies classes.

Second, volunteer work will help your child become more keenly aware of situations that are often the result of a lack of education   Many social ills are directly related to a lack of schooling or a lack of information or a lack of awareness. Most not-for-profit agencies and organizations deal with problems that need to be solved—in other words, potential research projects. Encourage your volunteering teen to think about ways in which problems might be alleviated or remedied.

What Type of Volunteer Work?   Encourage your child to come along with you as *you* volunteer. If your church has a clothing program for the homeless, get involved in the program with your child. If you take on the job of circulating a collection envelope in your neighborhood, helping with the food co-op, or building a house or

cleaning up a yard or doing repairs for someone, find a niche for your teen in the project. Don't send your teen out to volunteer when you aren't also volunteering. Volunteer together. You'll learn together and, in the process, learn more about each other as parent and child!

43 • Strengthen Your Child's Memory

Memorization is a learning *skill*. It can be developed.

Repetition   Most memory work is a matter of repetition. Generally speaking, a person needs to rehearse information to himself at least seven times so that the information can be filed in long-term memory to be recalled later. This concept is at the heart of what we call study. Studying a body of material, essentially, is reviewing it until a person has confronted it a sufficient number of times to remember it.

Find ways to rehearse information with your child. Sing the alphabet song as you run errands around town. Quote a Scripture verse repeatedly through a day. Use a new vocabulary word in as many contexts as you can while you are grocery shopping with your child.

Association   To enhance recall ability, your child can imagine a picture to go along with the concept or words being memorized. For example, if she is attempting to memorize 1492 as the year in which Columbus landed in the Caribbean, she might mentally visualize the numbers 1, 4, 9, and 2 as the shapes of four islands in the sea.

Aural association is also helpful: "In 1492, Columbus

sailed the ocean blue," or "*I* before *E* except after *C.*"
Encourage your child to make up a sentence with all the
facts in it that he wants to memorize or, better yet, to
come up with a poem.

Organization   Information is easier to memorize if it
is first outlined. Another effective approach is to put it in
some type of order that makes sense to the learner or can
be associated with other words and ideas. For example,
"every good boy does fine" helps children learn the
names of the notes E-G-B-D-F that go on the lines in a
treble clef staff.

Exercise   The memory is a little like a muscle—the
more people do memory work, the easier it seems for
most to commit something to memory. As a general principle, you can help your child memorize school-related
information by encouraging her to memorize nonschool-
related information. If your child is interested in baseball,
suggest that she memorize baseball facts. Scripture
verses, poems, and short famous passages of literature
(such as the Gettysburg Address, paragraphs from Shake-
speare, and so forth) are a memory challenge that may or
may not relate directly to the curriculum but will relate to
the ability to memorize school-related information.

Fun   Make memory work fun for your child. Don't
force him to memorize; rather, challenge him. Children
truly enjoy committing songs to memory—from "The
Twelve Days of Christmas" to camp songs to the alphabet
song. Tongue twisters are another fun way to develop
memory skills, and they also improve enunciation.

44 • Practice a Second Language

Is your child learning a second language in school? Practice it at home! Of course, you must be willing to learn the language along with your child—at least the key phrases and words.

You can usually incorporate practice in the general flow of your life as a family. For example, at the dinner table, ask your child to pass the *brot* instead of the bread. If you're looking for a book, ask your child, "¿Donde esta el libro?"

Tape Sets Encourage your child to learn the language. There's a big difference between knowing enough Spanish to score a passing grade and knowing how to speak the language. Always encourage your child to learn more than what is required in the school course, especially when it comes to languages.

Excellent foreign language tape sets are available. Listen to them with your child from time to time. Practice saying phrases back and forth to each other.

Shared Secret Approach language learning with your child as something of a "secret code." The language becomes a secret language you are learning to share, a necessity if you are ever to spy out a foreign land (in a friendly manner) or truly to be successful in dealing with people who speak only that language. By making language acquisition something of a game, many children are freed to try new sounds and combinations of words, and as a result, they actually become conversant in the second language in a much shorter time.

Opportunities to Speak the Language   You probably don't need to travel very far to give your child an opportunity to try out his newly learned language skills—perhaps only a subway ride into an ethnic neighborhood, a visit to an ethnic restaurant, or a conversation with someone who comes into your home and is a native speaker of another language. If your child is learning Spanish, you might even encourage occasional viewing of the Spanish channel on television. If you live in New England, try tuning in a French-speaking radio station broadcast from Quebec.

Valuing a Second Language   Let your child know—by statement and by example—that you value the ability to speak more than one language. Explain why.

- People who study languages tend to improve their general communication skills—listening, speaking, and writing.

- The study of a foreign language frequently causes students to study their own language with greater interest and with a greater concern for correct grammar, vocabulary, pronunciation, and the elimination of filler phrases such as "and um."

- The ability to speak a second language will become increasingly relevant as our economy becomes more global in perspective and the foreign-language-speaking populations of our own nation increase.

45 • Invite Interesting Adults into Your Home

Do you have friends who have traveled extensively? Are well read? Are good conversationalists? Have lived abroad or are from another nation or area of the country?

Do you have friends who are experts in their fields? Do you have a friend with unusual hobbies, interests, or skills?

Invite your interesting adult friends over to dinner from time to time, and include your child in the encounter. Allow her to be a part of the conversation. Encourage her to ask questions that will bring out the uniqueness of your guest:

- "What was it like when _____ ?"

- "How did you feel when _____ ?"

- "What was your most exciting adventure?"

- "How did you become interested in _____ ?"

- "Where did you learn to _____ ?"

Your child will learn how to converse—which includes asking intelligent questions, which in turn is a school-valued skill. Your child will have his horizons broadened in a way that you or his teacher might not be able to broaden them. Your child will learn that not all adults are alike. He'll grow in his appreciation for people with different skills, talents, abilities, experiences, and backgrounds.

Creating Encounters You may say, "But I don't know any people who are different from us or who have unusual or intriguing backgrounds, experiences, or abilities." Here are three opportunities to consider:

1. Take your child to guest lectures, especially to travelog programs that might include films of exotic places. Introduce yourselves to the presenter afterward. Discuss with your child a question or two he might ask. Most presenters, no matter how famous, are thrilled to spend a few moments talking to a child.

2. Invite missionary friends or guest speakers at your church to go out to lunch or dinner with you. Beforehand, read about the nation in which they have been working.

Frame some questions to ask. Your child can always ask, "What is it like for the children where you are a missionary?"

3. Sometimes family members are more interesting than we give them credit for being. Have your child "interview" Grandma and Grandpa about what life was like when they were your child's age. Let her play journalist, complete with tape recorder or video recorder. Work out some questions to ask in advance.

Invite relatives to tell their favorite stories or adventures. You might be surprised at what you *didn't* know about your family members!

46 • Schedule Aptitude Testing

Parents frequently see in their children the traits and abilities they *want* to see. Thus, parents may expect their children to become something, do something, or win something that the children don't want or are incapable of attaining.

Children frequently focus on what they *cannot* do rather than on their successes or strengths. This emphasis can lead to low self-esteem and a "give up" attitude toward future success.

Showing the Way A way to circumvent both problems is to provide aptitude testing for your children at fairly early ages, preferably no later than the early teen years.

Aptitude testing reveals to you and your child her inherent abilities and helps her envision possible career paths—and the necessary educational paths for reaching career goals. Aptitude testing can give your child

- a sense of self-worth. Your child has abilities and a unique role to fill on this earth.

- direction. Your child can begin to answer the questions, "What do I want to do with my life? Why am I here? What is my future?"

• hope. Your child can be successful and have a bright future.

Finding the Tests Most junior high and high schools offer aptitude testing opportunities. In some cases, you'll need to seek out these tests from a guidance counselor. In other cases, you may want to contact an educational consultant or a psychologist to determine where and when you can schedule aptitude tests for your child.

Another possibility is to contact a college placement office. These offices generally have aptitude tests available for self-testing. You may need to spend a few dollars for the test and its analysis, but the money is well worth it. (You may save thousands of dollars in college tuition spent while your college student "discovers" a major through trial and error.)

One of the most reliable and thorough tests is that constructed by Johnson & O'Connor, which has lab testing sites in several major U.S. cities. These tests focus on very specific skills, and they usually reveal the three to five aptitudes in which a person scores most highly; aptitude combinations point toward very specific career possibilities. This particular test is expensive, but again, it may be one of the most sound investments you ever make in helping your child prepare for adulthood.

47 • Play Games and Work Puzzles

All games and puzzles teach, even those that may seem rather mindless or a matter of luck. They teach a child

- how to take turns.

- how to identify the role of luck and the role of skill.

- how to win and how to lose.

Puzzles—from Rubik's cubes to jigsaw puzzles—teach your child about spatial relationships and logic. Most problems are solved in a way very similar to the way puzzles are put together: clustering of similar pieces, getting a sense of the big picture, finding relationships that fit (person to person, person to task, task to task).

These lessons are inherent to the process of playing games and working puzzles. Beyond that, games and puzzles can help your child develop very specific learning skills.

Word Skills Choose games that help your child build vocabulary and develop spelling skills, such as Scrabble (or Scrabble Junior), Password, Boggle (or Boggle Junior), Wheel of Fortune, or Hangman.

Math and Logic Skills Checkers, chess, dominoes, most card games (such as Uno and Rook), and even ticktacktoe require logic. Stratego and Sorry! are logic games, as are Risk and Castle Risk.

Perception and Memory Skills The Where's Waldo? games (and puzzles and books), Memory Cards, and various types of matching games and puzzles develop perception and memory skills. A number of "you figure it out" games and puzzles are also available, some in book form, such as the You Be the Jury and You Be the Detective series. Where in the World Is Carmen Sandiego? challenges memory and logic skills as well as a knowledge of geography.

Life Skills Some games help a child learn how to deal with various aspects of life—such as role-modeling games and games such as Monopoly (or Children's Monopoly) or Allowance.

School Facts Children enjoy playing with Speak & Read, Speak & Spell, and Speak & Math games, as well as Little Professor, all of which reinforce the learning of memorized facts. Go to the Head of the Class, Junior Trivia, and Jeopardy are fact-based games that test a player's knowledge in various areas.

Flash Cards Children frequently think of flash cards as games. Brain Quest provides sets of cards by grade level for your child to use in testing his own knowledge of general school subjects.

Puzzle Books   Mazes, dot-to-dot puzzles, crosswords, jumbled letter, secret code, and hidden picture puzzles assist in developing basic learning and school skills of perception, logic, spelling, and fact association.

The best news of all, of course, is that children like to play games and work puzzles. The learning reinforced by games and puzzles is virtually painless.

Lighten Up!

Learning can be fun. And sometimes fun things result in learning. Don't limit your child's school-related activities to topics or formats that are serious or structured. Instead, encourage your child to

- tell jokes or ask riddles. You'll foster communication skills and reading skills, and your child won't even realize it.

- make up stories. Not lies—but creative stories. Let your child develop plot lines, and ask him to describe characters and places. Encourage the development of dialogue. Again, you will help build communication skills.

- design something. Perhaps a car, a theme park ride, or a wallpaper border.

- make up puns. This is a great way to develop her vocabulary!

- interview people. He can start with family and friends. He will have fun playing reporter while learning a lot about how to conduct research.

- ask "what if?" questions. Let her imagination wander from the serious to the absurd! You'll be surprised how much science information is called into play.

48 • Choose Toys that Teach Well

All toys teach. The challenge to parents is to find toys that teach the values—and provide opportunities for children to learn the lessons and acquire the skills—that parents want their children to have!

You, as a parent, have the prime responsibility for choosing your child's toys. Don't leave the choice to your child any more than you would leave the decision about her nutrition up to her.

Choose toys that

- promote a constructive expression of feelings and ideas. Too many toys are aimed at violence and destruction. Instead, choose toys that foster positive socialization—for example, toy trucks over toy guns.

- call upon your child's imagination. Avoid toys linked to cartoons or movies. These toys feature characters that already have well-developed roles and prescribed patterns of behavior and relationships. A toy that is "media free" allows your child to give character traits to a figure and to come up with new and original scenarios for it. Most of your child's toys should be child powered, not battery powered.

- put your child into motion. Trikes and bikes, pounding toys and swing sets, Frisbees and balls—all put your child into motion to develop large-motor skills. Such toys actually teach a sense of balance, eye-hand coordination, and the basic principle "for every action there is a reaction."

- give your child an opportunity to put things together. Construction sets (from Legos to Tinkertoys) and many craft kits allow your child to learn combining skills, many of which provide lessons in sequencing, spatial relationships, and general principles of balance and design.

Art and craft kits enhance your child's "art" education and creativity as well as eye-hand coordination and left-brain, right-brain synthesis. Science kits—such as bug boxes, flower presses, bird feeders, chemistry sets, weather sets, crystal-growing sets, miniature greenhouses, ant farms, and solar and wind power experimental sets—reinforce what your child is learning in science classes.

49 • Make Something Together

Find a project that you and your child can make together.

It may be building a playhouse, treehouse, or outdoor playset.

It may be making a dollhouse, putting together a model airplane, or nailing together a birdhouse.

It may be stitching a dress, making a costume, or decorating a sweatshirt.

You may want to take on the challenge of fixing up an old car together or redecorating your child's room in a way that is mutually satisfactory.

All of these projects can reinforce basic school skills:

- Dividing a task into subtasks

- Sequencing or prioritizing subtasks

- Reading and following instructions

- Measuring correctly

- Making and following a budget

Such projects call upon your child's imagination, develop your child's cooperation skills, and reinforce eye-hand coordination.

Finish What You Start Put yourself and your child under the discipline of finishing the task that you have started. You'll give a boost to your child's self-esteem and confidence and teach your child the importance of follow-through.

A Real Challenge Undertake a project that is something both you and your child *want* to do. Also strive to find a project that represents a real challenge. One family decided to build a summer cabin. They took five years to complete the task, but every family member had a vital role in the building process. The resulting cabin is truly a cherished "home away from home" for each person.

Another family decided to convert the attic into a bedroom for the elder son. Even the younger son—also with a desire for a room of his own—was happy to pitch in and help!

One family carved out a series of putting greens in their backyard, complete with a sand trap and water hazard.

One father and son restored an old car to tip-top running condition and appearance. They spent many hours working under the hood together in anticipation of the day when the son could drive the car as his own.

Through such tasks, parents and children communicate, solve problems together, and pass on skills from one generation to the next. They are vital, valuable, and vibrant learning opportunities!

50 • Let Your Child Help with Household Chores and Repairs

Let your child help you fix up or repair the old things in your lives. Most of the learning skills are the same in building new and repairing old—skills related to reading, math, logic, and organization of information and tasks.

Possible Lessons from History Repairing or refinishing antique furniture, toys, tools, and other items leads easily to the questions, "How was this used? Why was this made this way? How would this be done or manufactured differently today? What time period is this from and how do we know?" Encourage your child to read up on old items that you are fixing. You'll reinforce reading and research skills and add to your child's understanding of history and culture.

Memory In taking an item apart for cleaning or repair, one must remember where each piece went and how it fit with the other pieces to put the item back together.

Ingenuity and Creativity Many times, a missing part or piece for an old item must be made rather than purchased. Problem-solving skills are brought into play, as are principles of math and design and skills related to measuring and researching.

Let your child help you replace a worn-out washer in a faucet, change a fuse, hang the storm windows, or repair the sagging step. You'll pass on significant life skills to your child and discuss some basic principles of physics as they apply to real life.

Chores   Encourage your child to help you with household chores. In meal preparation, for example, your child can read recipes, follow directions, see mathematical principles and proportions as he measures ingredients, and witness chemical reactions involved in combining ingredients and subjecting them to heat or cold.

As you do chores together—such as cleaning, yard work, or laundry—talk to your child about the way these chores were done in the past, pointing out the value of certain inventions and procedures that have been developed in the past hundred years. Ask your child, "What do you suppose doing this chore will be like thirty years from now? What new inventions might we have that will make this chore easier, accomplished more quickly, unnecessary, or better for the environment?" Prick your child's curiosity and spark his imagination. Who knows what your child might invent!

In repairing the old and doing the mundane, your child learns an extremely valuable lesson about learning itself: it never ends. The body of information we know as "fact, concept, and principle" is ever expanding.

51 • Provide Opportunities for Your Child to Teach

To be a successful teacher, one must first know the material. To determine if your child truly has learned a task, skill, or body of facts—or to motivate your child to do so —make your child the teacher.

Playing School Encourage your child at an early age to play school with other children. Provide a chalkboard and chalk. Some models come with an easel or a magnetic board.

Small desks and child-size typewriters, pads of ruled newsprint, and pencils that fit small fingers are all items that promote school play.

Child-to-Child Tutoring Encourage your child to share his skills and information with his siblings and peers. If your child knows how to tie his shoes, let him teach a younger brother or sister that skill. If your child passed geometry with flying colors, hire him to tutor a younger sibling who may be struggling with the subject. Encourage your teenager to volunteer in a literacy program to teach children how to read or to teach foreign students how to speak English.

Showing Off Skills From time to time, ask your child to teach you something.

- "Show me" how this works, how to play this computer game, how to solve this puzzle.

- "Help me" get up to speed with the current fashions, put together an outfit for the occasion at hand, understand the lyrics to the rap you've been listening to all afternoon.

- "Teach me" new words, new technologies, new tips and techniques.

Research Projects You may want to ask your child to help you with some research that you need but don't have time to do. For example, ask your teen to research the safest, most reliable, and "best buy" automobile for under $15,000 or to research the best washing machine on the market or to figure out the best way to get to the store across town without running into road construction or traffic delays. Ask your child to give you her conclusions backed up with facts and details.

Special Interests As your child pursues his special interests and hobbies, urge him to share with you what he is learning or discovering. For example, if your child shows an interest in astronomy, have him point out certain constellations and stars. If your child is a bird-watcher, ask him to tell you the names of birds you see as you travel together.

Teacher Tips   Never put down your child for a lack of information. Rather, challenge her to continue her exploration. Do correct misinformation. Rather than say, "That's wrong," however, suggest that your child double-check the information, or say to your child, "That isn't the way I learned it. I may have learned it wrong. Can you show me your reference on that?"

Give your child the option of saying, "I goofed" or "I don't know." The honest teacher must admit to mistakes and inadequacies. The best way to encourage your child to own his mistakes is to admit your lack of knowledge or your errors. It's not a failure to "not know" or to "get it wrong"; it's a failure to continue not knowing or to refuse to find the right or better answers. Furthermore, a teacher will never know it all. Always encourage your child to keep learning and keep teaching.

52 • Be Your Child's Biggest School Fan

Be a parental cheerleader for your child's school. Your child will strive harder to score educational success and will give a better effort to the process. In so doing, she is likely to achieve more than she would *without* your encouragement from the sidelines.

Support Events   Attend school performances, especially if your child is performing, but even if your child isn't on stage. Be there to support choir concerts, plays, pageants, or school fairs.

Be quick to volunteer as a chaperone for school-related events or to help out with school social functions.

Lend your support to fund-raising drives for the school —walkathons, for example, to raise money for new playground equipment, or candy sales to buy new band uniforms.

Vote   Vote in school-related elections; vote on bond issues and legislative bills related to teachers and schools. Voice your opinion in support of schools and educational issues to your elected representatives. Even if you choose to vote against a tax measure or for a school board candidate who isn't elected, your participation in the process sends a strong signal to your child that schools and schooling are significant to you.

Wear the Colors Wear the colors of your child's school to his games.

If your child brings home a bumper sticker that points to her place on the principal's honor role or even a bumper sticker that presents the name of the school, "wear" it proudly on the family vehicle.

Know the words to the school song or alma mater for your child's school or the fight song for the teams.

All of these actions bear witness to your child that you regard school as a vitally important place and that you value the educational process within its walls. In being a fan of your child's school, you are being his fan, too. You are saying to your child, "I'm proud of your school affiliation and your school achievements."

Be a consistent fan, whether your child's school teams win or lose. The message that translates readily to your child is that you will be supportive of your child, regardless of her personal successes or failures, and that you will be her fan always.

Enhance Staying Power A child whose parent regards school as important is nearly always a child who regards school as important. Such a child rarely drops out of school. The longer your child stays in school and the more he values the process, the more he is likely to learn. The more he learns, the more he is likely to succeed—not only in school but in life.